Sell Like Crazy With 2020

Best Strategies for 2020 And Beyond

Table of Contents

This is to congratulate Mr. Keller Jnr and his team towards the efforts made to bring out the book on "Social Media Marketing Best Strategies for 2020 And Beyond". The book has all the strategies you need to grow your business online

Chapter 1: Introduction

In today's digital economy, practical business knowledge is more than powerful. It is essential for survival and elementary for thriving! And it is no different when you are looking for a social media marketing strategy for 2020. Online marketing has gone beyond likes rather focus on providing value.

Currently, Instagram is testing how removing likes from the public count affects the user experience. In a statement the company CEO Adam Mosseri says is an effort to promote mental health: "The idea is to try to depressurize Instagram, make it less of a competition, and give people more space to focus on connecting with the people they love and things that inspire them."

I think every other social media platforms should adopt this, particularly for business pages. Removing likes should also help eliminate fraud and fake followers— people who pay for likes.

Likes mean very little because they are rarely a good indicator of success. For any advanced social media marketer, you measure things like traffic to your website, leads, and purchases that came as a result of your effort on those platforms.

As a marketer, if you follow your metrics closely, you will know that thousands of likes doesn't guarantee these things.

What this does mean though, is that you will want to worry less about the vanity metrics and focus more on action-oriented results.

On the plus, getting rid of public likes put a heavier emphasis on quality rather than quantity, and should encourage brands and users to focus on creating attention-grabbing content that will drive action that goes beyond a double tap.

Are you a beginner who wants to build a domain on social media? I will advise you to get into the always-be-testing mindset. You don't necessarily have to be on every social media platform. But you should test them and see if it is where your audience is and if it can help attract new customers.

The reason why you need to test different platforms upon building your business is that social media isn't as straightforward as it used to be - from rolling out new updates such as tools for interactive video, customer service, analytics, artificial intelligence, visual search, and shoppable images to demographic studies. When you find the right channel, a succinct strategy will help your brand tackle its goals with a sense of purpose.

Chapter 2: Create Content On Platforms Where Attention Is Underpriced.

Joel Kaplan made a shocking revelation in 2017,

"3 weeks ago, I had zero followers on any of my social media platforms. Today, I have 447,000 views on Quora. My answers have been upvoted over 11,800 times. I even got published in Forbes."

Are you wondering how he managed to pull that off in such a short amount of time?
He used one of the most powerful strategies in social media marketing looked down by various online marketers. And that is to create content on platforms where attention is underpriced.

Unarguably, most people try to build their brands on extremely competitive platforms. We think since the platform is crowded, we will easily pick our audience and leave. Let me ask you if you started your social media marketing strategy now, do you think it would be easier to build your brand on Facebook or a new arising platform?

The answer is a new platform. Because you are not competing against hundreds and thousands of people for their attention. While there are many aspiring marketers on a new platform, there are many more people trying to be influencers on Facebook.

Aside from that, up and coming platforms want to increase engagement so they will end up showing your content to more and more people. That is why Kaplan's content was shown to over 447,000 people in just 21 days?

There are a couple of others who took this part to fame. Gary Vee published his first-ever Wine Library TV video on May 17th, 2006. Just imagine what YouTube popularity is back then. If I may ask, which of you or relative streams YouTube videos in 2006? I bet very scanty people did. Take a look at Gary Vaynerchuk now, he is blown and living out his dreams.

Have you heard of Logan Paul? An American YouTuber. He followed this simple strategy when Vine was just taking off and I believe today, you know where consistency and creating content on platforms where attention is underpriced has gotten him today.

What of Nicholas Cole, a writer and columnist for Inc Magazine, and Top Writer on Quora. Today, his work has been published in TIME, Forbes, Fortune, Entrepreneur, The Huffington Post, Business Insider, and more.

Guessing where he started? Quora. He started writing on Quora in 2014 back when the platform was just starting and didn't have many writers. Now, he has over 22 million views on Quora aside been featured on the aforementioned platforms.

There's another chap worthy of note. Julius Dein. If you are a Snapchat enthusiast, not many people use the platform then, I believe. The few who did know this guy, the magician. He started doing magic tricks on Snapchat when the platform was just beginning to take off. He now has 2.8 million followers and travels the world doing magic.

Want a social media marketing strategy that will build you a massive following and make you an influencer? Create content on platforms where attention is underpriced, and you will live to testify in a short time like Joel Kaplan and others.

Chapter 3: Set Goals That Make Sense for Your Business

As you look back over this year, how happy are you with your business's performance? Are you patting yourself on the back, having nailed every goal? Smiling as you look over your long list of milestones achieved? Resting on your laurels?

If the answer is no, then you are like many business owners who have trouble hitting their business targets. You know exactly what you want—a bigger business, larger per-customer sales, more leads, higher profits—but you struggle to meet your goals.

Well-chosen goals and objectives point a new business in the right direction and keep an established company on the right track. Because coming up with a social media plan means having an end-game in mind.

Whether your goal is to make more money from your existing customers or amping up your reach with new followers, manage your finances, streamline your processes, and motivate your employees—all at the same time. It is totally up to you to get all things done by setting realistic social media goals.

Knowing your SWOT (strengths, weaknesses, opportunities,

and threats) analysis is a fantastic way to be crystal clear about what needs to be addressed first in your business. Hence, I recommend tackling smaller objectives that allow you to scale your social efforts in a way that is both reasonable and affordable.

Chapter 4: Generate Leads and Sales

Lots of people want to hear from your business, and the audiences want to be notified about new products or promos. Whether online or in-store, they aren't going to make social purchases by accident, you need to alert them.

Facebook lead ads make the lead generation process easy. People can simply tap your ad and a form pops up. This form covers their Facebook contact information and ready to be sent directly to you with ease even on the small screen.

All you are required to get higher-quality leads is to customize your forms to ask for the most important information first. Then with just a few taps, the potential customers can get the information they want, and you generate a qualified lead for your business.

During this process, I would advise newly generated leads to be synced directly with your CRM, (Customer Relationship Management) as there are plenty of CRMs both free and paid you can incorporate into your lead generation journey so your sales team can take immediate action.

Lead ads can take many forms. Depending on the target audience, you can make it in the form of quote or demo requests, newsletter subscriptions, event registrations, and more.

Chapter 5: Steps to Generating Lead Ads and Sales

Add custom questions

Address your question when drafting your lead ads so you can uncover the potential audiences' preferences, and ensure that you are reaching out to the correct people with the right information.

Use dynamic ads for lead generation

When setting your lead generation ads, center your message on what people have previously expressed interest in. By retargeting those customers and sending them directly to a lead form, you have the opportunity to collect higher-quality leads.

Implement the dealer locator.

People are still using store locators despite the existence of Google Maps and business and food directory apps.

That's right—contrary to popular belief, customers still prefer your website for online information. In fact, having a store locator on your website is more than essential for any business for various reasons. And integrating it into your ad yields positive result.

As you know when customers are driven to buy something, time is of the essence. This is why once a potential customer completes a form to find out more, show them where the closest dealership is located.

On the whole, Facebook store locators are a great way to provide updated, relevant information to customers instantly. And to this day, it can become more than an address book.

Strategies That Will Help You Get Higher-quality Leads

Add a click-to-call option.

We need to be strategic when creating Facebook ads for our businesses. A few months ago, I stumbled on a digital marketing institute ad on Facebook. Their ads target were to get students and even working-class to enroll in their institute, but they weren't strategic enough in their lead generation ads creation.

What do I mean?

It should be once someone has completed a form, allow them to call your office straight away to start a conversation. But that wasn't the case here.

Instead, they collect phone numbers and start calling in after a week to two weeks. In case you are wondering how I know this, I purposefully filled the form to know how it would end.

And like I predicted earlier, they called in and I already forgot

I ever filled a form to enroll in a digital marketing institute. Which I believed others must have forgotten too.

Allow people to book with appointment scheduling.

Don't wait to send a follow-up email or place a call to determine a customer's preferred appointment time and date. Once someone has filled in your form, they can also indicate when would be best of them to meet, decreasing the number of follow-ups needed.

Just imagine if that digital marketing institute had created their lead ad in a way that lets interested persons fill in their preferred appointment time and date.

There won't be the need to collects hundreds of phone numbers and start calling one after the other. Very saddening is that most of the people may not really be interested in your digital marketing class.

But when your lead generation ad allows people to book with appointment scheduling, you will save cost and time. Your lead ad will look professional and attract more people who are really interested in your business.

Create higher-intent lead forms.

Although it looks so easy and straightforward based on how I'm breaking it bits by bits, but, Facebook lead ads being increasingly common tool for marketers, might take a bit of work to set up, but can yield great results by providing a good user experience for your potential customers.

Adding friction to the form, such as a review screen or slide to submit button, will help acquire leads that might have a higher level of intent and interest in your product.

Prospects confirm their details on the review screen after reading the privacy policy. This can reduce lead volume, helping to sift out low-quality leads while maintaining the mobile optimization of the forms and a user-friendly experience.

Make Your Lead Ads Stand Out

One of the most important points when creating your Facebook lead ad is making it engaging. Facebook has made it easier for you to reach the right people through your lead ad, but how can you guarantee that those 'right people' won't just scroll straight past it? Your ad's first impression counts. It must be appealing and relevant to the potential customer.

How? Facebook understands that there are little differences in styles and approaches to a specific industry, and creates custom features for lead ads with business in mind.

Show your ad's value.

Your ad should clearly communicate why it's valuable for people to share their information with your business. For an automotive lead ad, there is the help of dealer locator so that people can find nearby dealerships, as well as indicating a date and time preference to set up a test drive.

For an education-based lead ad, it enables you to use custom questions to generate your interest forms for your different courses and programs.

For people with intents to creating a business-to-business lead ad, there is the click-to-call that makes it simpler for potential clients to contact you straight away to learn more without delay.

While for CPG lead ads, it is best to display information about relevant products to current and potential customers and allow them to sign up for a newsletter or request a sample.

But collecting that information isn't always easy—getting someone to provide your company with their data isn't easy—so it's important to make the sign-up process as simple as possible by asking as few questions as possible and ensure the ad reflect the brand in question.

Chapter 6: Over-saturated market place: Scope to Help You Standout

Branding is essential in a world saturated by companies competing in the same market sector. Your brand must stand out from the competition as brand recognition has a significant impact on buying behavior.

In today's hectic technology-driven world, people process a lot of information daily from social media, TV, the radio, billboards, posters, social media, the internet, smartphones, tablets, newspapers, cinema, and many more.

Thus, small businesses and big corporations alike can do much to build and maintain their brand recognition, to be "top of mind" with customers who are ready to buy online or in the store.

Using a unique, touching, or heartfelt story that lets customers know why it's in business makes it easier for users to identify your brand in the pool of others because customers tend to remember brands that reach them on a personal or emotional level.

Another way to build and maintain brand recognition is by providing exemplary customer service. Customers are more likely to recommend and buy products from a company they know values their patronage.

Those who truly want to outsmart their competitors in the online businesses should also aim to exceed their customers' expectations and also seek to aim to do something extraordinary like educating their customers on products and services to stiffen seller to buyer relationship.

Create Brand Awareness

According to HubShot, "Your brand identity is the representation of your company's reputation through the conveyance of attributes, values, purpose, strengths, and passions."

In 2020, companies have devised another strategy to creating authentic and lasting brand awareness, and that is to avoid solely publishing promotional messages. Instead, focus on content that emphasizes your personality or values first.

Think creatively by developing a unique brand identity which one of the surest ways in increasing your brand's awareness.

For example, Dollar Shave Club, a brand known for being witty with their ad, started one of their ad title, "Our Blades Are F**king Great," the video that introduced the brand was comical and outrageous. In a short time, they gained millions of views on YouTube through social shares.

And the most interesting fact of the viral video ad is that 12,000 people signed up for the service within some hours of the video's launch. I shared this as a secret so you can incorporate this idea in to your own ideas or campaigns.

Sincerely, you don't have to be Dollar Shave Club or anyone to be able to create a unique ad or campaign that will leave an impression with your audience. Think out of the box and develop content around your selling point.

Content that tells a story of who you are; an ad that connects with your brand in some personal way—then your audience will be more likely to share your content, which in turn will give your sales a boost.

Make timeliness a top priority

"I do not feel appreciated or valued as he does not return my calls or emails, or when he does it is days or weeks later. Does he think what I do is not important?"
"My boss doesn't get back to me."
"Our senior leaders seldom respond to us. It seems they take us for granted."

Everyone wants to feel appreciated and valued.
Staff desire timely responses to their queries.
Customers want their questions answered irrespective of the time it's been asked.

The ugly truth remains that you can't always expect customers to operate on "your time." Likewise, it's crucial to be able to reach and respond to followers on time.

How do you joggle them together?

16

You might see some recommending times to post late in the evening, for example. But if your brand isn't there to communicate, what's the point of posting at the "preferred" time?

Instead, try to ensure your social media or community managers are available and ready to answer any product questions or concerns when you tweet or post. It's smart to learn the best times to post on social media. However, it's just as critical to engage after posting.

Another thing to consider is keeping a speedier response. The core element of marketing is maintaining a speedy attention. Any business will tell you that retaining customers is easier than acquiring new ones.

And, it can be at least five times more costly to acquire a new customer than to keep one, which is why brands ensure conversations or engagement opportunities aren't left unattended.

The advantage of keeping speedier responses and maintaining meaningful conversations regularly is that you gain respect as a brand by just being present and talking to your audience. That's why social customer care is so important to brands wanting to increase consumers' awareness.

Whether it's capitalizing on a compliment or responding to a question, businesses shouldn't leave customers hanging. Through the right social media monitoring tools, you can find instances across all your channels to interact, respond and gauge customers around-the-clock.

Grow your brand's audience.

No marketer is ever satisfied with a specific number of followers. Evident why big brands like Nike, Apple, Samsung, Coca-Cola, Mercedes-Benz, McDonald's, Disney, and many more run ads and employ best hands in managing their social media presence, despite the authority and trust they've garnered to millions of followers they've acquired.

We all need new followers. It triggers a spot in ourselves that tell that our products and services are truly okay for public consumption. It also makes us feel like somewhat kinds of a strategist who knows how to lure the people into making the best choices, hence we feel accomplished and mentally high.

It also means finding ways to introduce your brand to folks who haven't heard of you before. So you need to imbibe efficient social media targeting using monitoring tools and utilizing specific keywords, phrases, or hashtags to reach your core audience much faster.

Increase community engagement.

You wouldn't want to lose your current followers, right? There's a local proverb that says, "A bird in hand is worth millions in the bush." I would advise you to find ways to grab your customers' attention and keep the bellows fanning the fire that fuels the successful strategies.

This means experimenting with messaging and content. For example, does your brand support holding contests, hashtags, and user-generated content? If so, use them.

Those are some of the simplest strategies that can help increase your engagement rate. Your audiences will turn your best cheerleaders if you are making them feel acknowledged by giving them something worthy to do.

Increase web traffic.

Are you laser-focused on generating leads or traffic to your website? Social media has the potential to create a huge impact on your traffic. This is a very easy and direct way to drive customers to your website through promotional posts or social media ads.

Monitor your conversions and URL clicks to help you better determine your Return On Investment from social media. Effectively incorporating any of these explicit goals is fair game and can help you better understand which networks to tackle, too.

When in doubt, keep your social media strategy simple rather than muddling it with too many objectives that might distract you.

Chapter 7: Research Your Target Audience through rich and industry specific content

Creating rich and industry-specific content for your product is an ideal solution to remain relevant in ever-changing online marketing, but distribution is undoubtedly its all-important path to success.

You can spend all the time and money in the world getting a wordsmith to produce the best content, but it all goes to waste if it fails to reach the right audience. And you wouldn't dare make assumptions of your chances because that itself is a more dangerous game.

So, before you invest all that effort, time, and resources on your marketing materials, it's a good idea to determine your target audience, find out how to effectively reach them, and figure out if they find your content appealing using the sheer wealth of demographic data and social media analytics tools out there, you really don't have much to think about.

So much of what you need to know about your audience to influence your social media marketing strategy is already out in the open. Take a look at today's demographics to identify who needs your product or service and who are most likely to buy it.

The data paints a basic image of your buyer persona's day-to-day tasks, activities, and buying decisions—allowing you to be familiar with your core customers so you can be able to determine which networks your brand should approach and what types of content to produce. Again, this is done to concentrate your message on the people who will make the most impact.

Study and follow these key ideas:

According to Bridget Kulla, Senior Digital marketing manager, "Having all our analytics under one roof really helps us be more effective and efficient in testing out content. It's so much easier to hone in on the types of content that work best for us, whether it's by channel, by time or something."

It is hard to imagine life without social media. There are platforms to fit just about anyone's lifestyle, making posting, tweeting, liking and friending daily mantras. But you should also know that no platform is one-size-fits-all.

Whether you are a seasoned social media marketer, a marketer looking to venture into social media marketing, or a business owner looking to leverage on social media, you should know that Facebook and YouTube are both prime places for ads due in part to their high-earning user bases.

Instagram is the emotional member of this social media family and since its purchase in 2012, Instagram continues to rise in popularity.

It is an engaging social media platform that allows users to express themselves with real experiences and create genuine interactions without distractions, keeping users focused on the eye-popping content that oozes with personality.

As of 2020 according to Statista, 35% of US teens rate Instagram as their favorite social network, second only to Snapchat. In terms of gender, 43% of women use Instagram while 31% of men use it.

Pinterest also has a wide international user base but its user-ship currently skews more heavily towards women; which is noted to boast the highest average order value for social shoppers. For example, in the US, it is said that 15% of men use Pinterest while 42% of women do.

LinkedIn's demographics favor those with professional careers. Perhaps reflecting the busy schedules of this more niche audience, daily usage is less frequent than Facebook and Instagram.

However, being a platform for the more educated folks makes it a hub for in-depth, industry-specific content that might be more complicated than what you see on Facebook or Twitter.

Although the demographics data above gives you insight into each channel, what about your own customers? This is more of a general analysis than niche-based.

Further analysis needs to be done before you can truly know your customer demographics on social media. That is why many brands use a social media dashboard which can provide an overview of who's following you and how they interact with you on each channel.

Chapter 8: Over-rule with Curated and Created Social Content

Content curation is the bread and butter of social media marketing. Meaning your social media marketing strategy is obviously centered on great content.

If you have weighed and find the platform that best suits your brand, you should have a pretty good idea of what to publish based on your goal and brand identity. There is no limit to what content you can develop. That means infographics, videos, blogs, posts, presentations are all fair game.

What does engaging social content look like and how do you make it happen? Creating engaging social media content requires a special approach. It must be unique, exciting, appealing, useful, concise, easy-to-understand, and actionable.

Moreover, to create something appealing that will make the audience stay on your page for a minute means you have to stick to content themes. Content themes are great to keep your social media feed consistent, colorful and aesthetically pleasing.

However, one of the toughest challenges to visual content is creating it on a day-to-day basis. Most brands struggle to keep to the pace on their own which is the reason they turn to using curated content to consistently keep highly-visual content. Even though others manage to handle it themselves.

Instagram is arguably the best channel for content themes given that it is totally visual. Sticking to a content theme has its numerous advantages, aside from the colorful and aesthetically pleasing feed, you will find it easier to develop your content calendar. For example, you might cycle between memes, product photos, and user-generated content while sticking to a rotating color scheme.

And if you are struggling to keep up with all the sources of social content, there are both free and paid social media management tools that can help you organize your media library and schedule your posts in advance.

To help narrow down the specifics of what you should be publishing and make sure you are developing innovative content, lookout on some social media trends to keep an eye on.

Also, don't forget to keep your salesy tactics to a minimum. As you can see, 57.5% of people found it annoying in this study on Sprout Social:

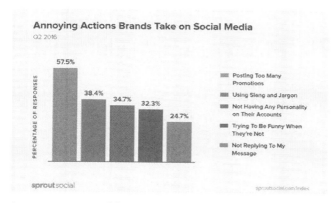

Annoying Actions Brands Take on Social Media
Q2 2016

57.5% — Posting Too Many Promotions
38.4% — Using Slang and Jargon
34.7% — Not Having Any Personality on Their Accounts
32.3% — Trying To Be Funny When They're Not
24.7% — Not Replying To My Message

sprout social
sproutsocial.com/index

Irrespective of how pleasing and highly-tuned your marketing style is, don't force your way in between your customers. Consumers find it offputting when brands and businesses post too many promotions. So be careful.

The secret sauce to getting your audience or customers to trust you is to show your human side and make them feel acknowledged rather than stuffing your products into their throats. Make them trust you first, and if they trust you – they will buy from you.

Alternatively, you can craft helpful content that people actually want to consume. Content that leads buyers to your products or services – without being pushy or salesy.

Stories and time-sensitive content

Tapping into your followers' FOMO (fear of missing out), Stories content on Instagram and Facebook is only going to become more important. Time-sensitive content is any visual content with a short life span that lasts for up to 24 hours. Users with FOMO (fear of missing out) can't afford to miss something interesting.

Popping up first in your followers' feeds by default, such content can help your brand's account "skip the line" and stay fresh in your audience's minds.

This is why, according to Tech Crunch, Facebook Stories, Snapchat and Instagram Stories are especially valuable for taking your followers behind-the-scenes and making your social feed feel a bit more personal.

For example, consider how you can use Stories to cover an event or take your followers on a journey without them having to leave the comfort of the gram.

However, as marketers know, content creation is time-consuming. Wasting valuable time and money to invest in ephemeral content that will disappear within 24 hours is a tough decision, but the gain is worth the time.

The reason to invest in time-sensitive content is that authenticity is at the top of your customers' minds.
While the number of paid ads, sponsored posts, and celebrity endorsements are growing at a faster rate, and a majority of the online users are saying authenticity is important to them when deciding which brands they support.

Hence, you should humanize your brand to earn customers' trust and loyalty, and time-sensitive content can help you achieve that goal.

Whether you are taking users behind the scenes or offering

something unique, time-sensitive content creates a sense of belonging, so followers feel special and understand who you are. When you humanize your company, you give your followers a clear reason to trust you.

Moreover, it is a way to stand out from a crowd of competitors who fight for the same target audience. Also, it encourages users to take action immediately because it is only available for a short period of time. And as the name implies, it saves time and effort.

Take advantage of video content in your strategy

Undoubtedly, video marketing is one of the potent additions to your promotion toolbox. You might still have your doubts. But it is really worth to consider using videos for promoting your business. Especially in social media marketing.

There are different ways to use video content in your social media strategy. But live videos appear to be all the rage right now and even if you don't have enough resources to create and use video content in your marketing, you have Facebook Live Videos and it doesn't require much. So, if you haven't already, it's time to jump on that bandwagon as soon as possible!

Here is a snapshot of a successful Facebook live by Caitlin Bacher:

Videos can make you some serious money. Adding a product video on your landing page can triple your conversion rate. And it also builds trust and lasting relationships which is the goal of content marketing.

This made Mark Schaefer, the Executive Director of Schaefer Marketing Solutions say: "The new era demands a focus on ignition, not just content, on trust, not just traffic, and on the elite people in your audience who are spreading and advocating your content."

Similarly, Facebook Live videos allow you to connect with your audience in an authentic way that isn't possible in other content formats. Plus you can repurpose your live videos. People can ask questions on-the-go, and your reply will make you look more human to them than a brand.

A combination of live videos and regularly recorded videos will be your best bet. Before you know it, you will have people flocking in your direction.

Chapter 9: You Can't Survive 2020 without the Right Tools

Are you really tired of guessing work? And you practically want to see your business sail in between the rumbles and hurdles of online marketing? Then tools are the right answer.

Tools make up the highest part of online marketing. From content posting to syncing your generated leads to analytics and so on. The tools you choose will determine the strength of your entire social media marketing strategy.

Think of it like building a home. If you began by putting up drywall or installing a deck without a steady foundation, it would fall to the ground. The same goes for your social media strategy. Finding the right tools will ensure your strategy runs effortlessly.

There are plenty of social media automation tools you can use to style and schedule your social content. And in every automation tool out there, there are three or more competing against each other that you can pick from depending on the needs and requirements of your business.

So are there loads of social media monitoring tools and analytics tools that can help you monitor your presence. Whether you use 1 or 5 tools comes down to personal preference, budget, and how serious you are about creating a cutting-edge social media marketing strategy.

Examples of a life-changing automation, monitoring and analytics tools you can use are Buffer, Hootsuite, Google Analytics, Serpstat, Netpeak Spider, Salesmate, Zoho Social, Sprout Social, Quintly, Sendible and hundreds of them out there that can help you manage almost every step of the social media marketing process.

Start a Facebook group

If you have ever thought about launching a Facebook group – now is the time. With the regular update occurring within social media – Facebook was hit the hardest. Facebook's algorithm changed, making Facebook pages more challenging to grow or profit from. No wonder it remains the most sought after platform for marketers.

Personally, I created two groups and joined over 15 Facebook groups to learn and reach more people and it has remained some of the best decisions ever. Facebook groups allow you to see more from your friends, family, and groups in your newsfeeds. And less "public content", such as from businesses or brands.

The benefits of creating a Facebook group are numerous. You can use it to increase your website traffic, promote your products and services in a non-salesy way, engage and connect with your audience in an authentic way, build your email list, grow your business and earn more money.

Launching or joining a Facebook group is a top-notch strategy to add to any social media marketing plan in 2020 and beyond.

Chapter 10: Off-Page SEO ranking factors

Off-page SEO, also known as off-site SEO, describes optimization techniques that can improve your ranking in search engine results pages (SERPs). The truth is creating awareness of your brand is how people come to know about your website. Hence, off-page SEOs are activities outside of your site and involve attracting links from other websites, shares on social media, and mentions across the web.

For example: You may form online communities and forums to contribute. Registering by filling your business details in local business directories. You may want to contribute by writing articles about your business on various other sites and educate the ones who are new to the field.

Contributing and enlightening the audience through various means available outside your page will help your business reach a wider audience and with links to reach into your business website or blog so they can learn more, a viral sensation about your business is achieved.

On the whole, this is an added advantage for your website ranking in Google because it tells search engines that your website is important to others on the web. Every link that you receive acts as an endorsement from another source that your website is quality.

Factors that demonstrate a strong Off-Page SEO presence include this:

Backlinks or Inbound Links

Links from other websites that direct users to your domain are termed as backlinks or inbound links. This lets external sources act as tie-breakers for websites that have the same quality of on-page SEO, and the part played by this is immense when considered in terms of Search Engine Optimization.

Are you wondering how?

It is a simple logic: Since the quantity and quality of the backlinks, a website has played a significant role in determining the ranking factor of that particular website, search engine credits such site highly. This is why you need to have quality backlinks from quality websites to help your website rank in Google Search.

For example, say that Company "Y" has a website that includes hundreds of On-Page SEO. That is each page is optimized for keywords, and the back-end code is written with the appropriate tags, page titles, and more.

Also, the same thing applies to Company "Z". It also has tons of On-page SEO. But with little difference which is that popular forums and local directories have linked to its site. Secondly, it has active social media accounts, and its CEO has been featured as an expert in the industry by other websites.

Judging by this, when Google search engine or any other search engine crawls Company "Y's" site and notes the relevancy of its On-Page SEO, but discovers that the Off-Page SEO is poor, Company "Z" by extension will earn a higher place in search engine rankings with its multiple backlinks, brand mentions, social media, publicity, and more. And that's what makes Off-Page SEO essential to any web page.

You see that links are a critical component to off-page SEO. It is important to be active in this Internet world by contributing, discussing, interacting, sharing and appreciating [especially in your domain].

It is a win-win strategy that helps you create more branding and it indirectly creates online referrals in-terms of backlinks. Which in turn helps your website rank higher in Google Search.

Note, before you start your off-page Seo campaign, trying to build backlinks is essential to understand the different types of links, as well as the factors that influence the equity of a link to your website.

Why?
Backlinks are of two types and one is more important than the other: No-Follow Backlinks and Do-Follow Backlinks. If you care about your website's performance in search engines, then knowing when and not to use do-follow and no-followed links isn't just important—it's crucial. However, when it comes to search engine optimization, there's a BIG difference between these two links.

No-follow Backlinks

These are links with a rel="nofollow" HTML tag applied to them. The nofollow tag tells search engines to ignore that link. Because nofollow links do not pass PageRank they likely don't impact search engine rankings. Although they give you the required traffic you might need to push your product or services but it's frowned at by Google.

Do-Follow Backlinks

Do-Follow backlinks are the exact opposite of No-Follow backlinks. These links not just bring in traffic but also helps in ranking a website in Google Search. Though these are considered worthy in terms of SEO, the qualities of these links vary. The quality of the backlink is measured in terms of the Page Rank it comes from.

Better the page rank, better the quality of backlink originating from it. So when you see the rel="external" is the indication denoting that the hyperlink is a do-follow backlink. Although sometimes it may not come with the rel attribute link, still, Google considers it as a Do-follow link.

As a user, it's impossible to tell the difference between a no-follow and do-follow link without going through the Page Source. You can click on, copy and use a no-follow link like any other link on the web. Right click on your browser and click "View page source". Next, look for the link in the HTML of the page. If you see a rel="no-follow" attribute, that link is no-followed. Otherwise, the link is do-follow.

However, all this no-follow and do-follow started when spammy sites started to rank really well in Google. This pushed high-quality sites out of the search results. Because the tactic worked so well, blog comment spam quickly spun out of control.

This triggered Google In 2005, to develop and roll out no-follow tag into their algorithm to curb the relevance of spammy backlinks; hence other search engines, Bing and Yahoo ultimately adopted it also.

This is the reason every website user should adopt backlink analysis. This is the process of critically analyzing the backlinks obtained for your website through certain software and tools. Analyze backlinks gotten from other websites, preferably your competitor's too. This method is practiced to get the quality and count of backlinks obtained, and to strategize a healthy campaign to obtain fruitful results.

Press Release Submissions

Marketing via press release is a very popular activity and one of the oldest techniques in the list. Any event within the company that is worth a grand announcement can be published as an Online Press Release such as a product's launch or an achievement in its field qualify to serve this purpose.

The real goal, however, is for journalists at those sites – be they newspapers or online journalists like Forbes – to cover your topic. And doing this well, you are getting attention to your business, building awareness, and getting people to check out what new product you have coming down the pipe. On the whole, Press release does not just supply you with an efficient backlink but also serves as a content which could reach a larger audience.

Blog Submission

Blogging is an important off-page optimization activity that can make your blog visible beyond the realms of your blogging circle. It is a method in which you submit blogs in blog submission sites, blog search engines, etc.

Maintaining a blog either within the website or through various other blogging websites like WordPress and Blogger.com helps you by generating various backlinks for your blog, earn a profit, and also to build a good rapport with potential customers, educate and update them which enhances your web traffic tremendously.

Since Blogger.com is a Google-owned subsidiary, preferring this would be a better option when compared to other blogging sites. Moreover, the benefits of blog submission include turning the website into a more approachable one. Allows for free brand awareness and expansion. In most cases, after reading the blog, many people are convinced to divert towards your official site and know more about you and your services.

Article Submissions

Unlike blog submissions, article submission is an off-page

activity where users and owners of the website actively post articles related to their website on the website of a third party. The main purpose behind article submission is to attract a large number of visitors (and links) to your website without incurring a great cost.

It is important to make sure that the articles you intend to submit are directly related or relevant to your business and should not be submitted in multiple sites, an additional point to be noted is that the article should be creative and interactive since it has the potential of bringing in a lot of visitors.

Directory submission

Directory submission is the term in which SEO experts try to reach business directory or industry directories and submit their business there with a link back to their website.

This is very popular, though most of the directories are spammy. But submitting your website on online directories that are renowned in your local online directory list still remains one of the principal methods to create an online presence.

Since directories are often searched for business-related queries by the users, registering with online directories expands the presence of your business. In addition to it, most blog directories are manually supervised for any wrong submissions.
Hence, these sites are spam free and are a potential source of building SEO friendly backlinks. Some directories also

provide dofollow backlinks. Imagine what benefit lies in getting the 10 do-follow backlinks from 10 submissions will have on your website's ranking in the search engine result pages

Forum Posting

This refers to generating quality inbound links by participating in online discussion forums. It allows you to post new posts and reply to old ones to drive traffic to your site. Forum comprises of contributors who are registered with the website forums).

These registered members can submit a topic for discussion called 'threads' and other members can comment, discuss, criticize and argue about various things as their way of contributing to the topic.

Being an expert in your field, advising and answering to questions related to your field using your business's name could attract many new customers and since the threads are saved for future purposes, your comments remain as a guide to newcomers.

Again, since the audience being targeted here are of the same field, conversions through your website can be expected when this method is performed efficiently. That is, when you can analyze a thread about your field in a way that pinches the forum users' pain-points and proffer solution to them, they will trace you to your website in search of more knowledge.

Community

If you are considering getting an online community forum and are wondering if it will help your website rank on search engine optimization the answer is yes. Creating communities on various social media platforms can enhance the engagement of your customers and could also proficiently increase the count of new customers.

However, social media platforms will not provide you with an SEO, rather, a brand community forum will. You might want to ask what I mean by a branded community? A branded community refers to a community that is hosted as an extension of the website.

Google+ being one of the subsidiaries of Google is an advantage and an ample importance to your services. When you build a community in it based on your product, the weightage it carries gives your website a real boost. Creating a community without better interaction won't do the trick.

Hence, hearing out to every community member and appealing to their doubts and necessities should be done regularly to move at the required pace. A greater advantage is that the articles and blog posts you publish could get a large audience when you showcase them in your community.

Classified Submissions

Classified submission is the method of posting your ad on various classified sites to promote your business brand, services, and products. There may be a handful of ways to submit your site online, but the classical and a still good and going way to submit your site is to try classified submission.

It is a cost-effective way to get targeted traffic and improve sales. There are huge numbers of classified sites that are available for free as well as on a payment basis and it remains a dominant method when advertising a product online.

Moreover, this concept is not new, but an advance form, when compared to earlier techniques of promotion and advertisement. Now one can promote one's own business over the internet with the help of online marketing locally and nationally.

PPT Sharing

PowerPoint presentations are a graphical way of approaching the audience. Professional presenters, salespeople, developers, designers, teachers, event spokespersons – We all love to share our business with a wider audience using a pictured format and through text to make them understand our businesses better.

However, live presentations are cool, but they impose evident limitations. Those 25 – 100 listeners in the room will enjoy the good vibes and a proper joke that come in a package with a nice presentation.

Yet there are thousands of people out there who didn't attend your class or event, but could make good use of your findings. More reason it is best to use PPT method which also favored setup by many slide hosting services across the internet.

You can convert this file to your desired format and share it over the internet through various presentation sites such as authorstream.com and slideshare.com to enable it to reach more people and effectively make them understand the business, even after months and years of creating the content.

Social bookmarking

Social bookmarking is a way for people to store, organize, search, and manage "bookmarks" of tagged web pages with a browser-based tool so that you can easily visit it again later. Instead of saving social media posts to your browser bookmarks, you can use different platforms' features to bookmark posts. Because the bookmarks are online, you'll be able to access them anywhere, from any device so far there is internet connection.

These bookmarks are usually public, and can be viewed by other members of the site where they are stored and also, very phenomenal in Search Engine Optimization (SEO) when combined with other link building strategies which will eventually contribute to high visibility and translate to higher traffic volumes and perhaps, higher conversion rate for the website. Meaning the more people who have access to your great content, the more likely that your content will go viral.

Bonus point: Anchor Text

Anchor text refers to the clickable words used to link one web page to another or Anchor Text is a keyword or phrase that links to a specific webpage. For example, in the below sentence, the Anchor Text is "How to Make Money Using Google Services in Amazon Store."

"For more details on How to Make Money Using Google Services, visit How to Make Money Using Google Services in Amazon Store." If you click on this Anchor Text, it takes you to the content link.

It is important to have a meaningful Anchor Text. Do not create "Click Here" as an Anchor Text. Anchor Text is the key for your SEO link building exercise. Search engines give more attention to Anchor Text to decide on your website ranking.

Social media marketing can be hard work. But the benefits are difficult to ignore. If you don' t take it seriously, you will undoubtedly miss out on leads, customers, online visibility, and sales.

Use these tactics to fine-tune your social media marketing strategy until you have created a winning strategy. Just remember, social networks are made for conversing with others. If you don' t make your audience a top priority – you won't see results.

About the Author

Simon Keller is a digital marketing expert who creates innovative campaigns for companies and publisher clients. He is a well-respected book publicist with a graphic design background that makes companies visual promotions and social media platforms pop.

He focuses much of his time on promoting companies through social media and creatively getting promotional material into the hands of tastemakers.

Printed in Great Britain
by Amazon